Andy Jackson
and the
Battles for New Orleans

BOOKS BY GRANT LYONS

Andy Jackson and the Battles for New Orleans
Tales the People Tell in Mexico

Andy Jackson and the Battles for New Orleans

by GRANT LYONS
Illustrated by PAUL FRAME

JULIAN MESSNER NEW YORK

Published by Julian Messner, a Division of Simon & Schuster, Inc.
A Gulf+Western Company
1 West 39 Street, New York, N.Y. 10018. All rights reserved.

Copyright © 1976 by Grant Lyons

Printed in the United States of America
Design by Marjorie Zaum

Library of Congress Cataloging in Publication Data
Lyons, Grant.
    Andy Jackson and the battles for New Orleans.

    Includes index.
    SUMMARY: Traces the events preceding and during the Battle of New Orleans where Andrew Jackson led the American troops to a decisive victory over the British.
    1. New Orleans, Battle of, 1815—Juvenile literature. 2. Jackson, Andrew, Pres. U.S., 1767-1845—Juvenile literature. [1. New Orleans, Battle of, 1815. 2. Jackson, Andrew, Pres. U.S., 1767-1845] I. Frame, Paul, 1913- II. Title.
E356.N5L86   973.5'239'0924   76-19078
ISBN 0-671-32802-6

Contents

CHAPTER

1. The *Chesapeake* Incident	7
2. A Second War for Independence	16
3. The Fortunes of War	22
4. New Orleans—The Paris of the New World	30
5. The Armada	42
6. The First Battle	48
7. "We Must Fight Them Tonight!"	53
8. The English Attack	59
9. The Great Cannon Duel	67
10. Field of Diamonds—Field of Blood	72
11. The Treaty of Ghent	81
12. After the Battles for New Orleans	86
Historical Places to Visit	91
Index	93

CHAPTER 1

The *Chesapeake* Incident

It was a bright sunny morning in June of 1807. Commodore James Barron, of the United States Navy, paced the upper deck of his new command ship, the *Chesapeake*.

It was going to be a beautiful day. Chesapeake Bay lay calm and blue, but there was a brisk wind for sailing. Slowly the port town of Hampton, Virginia slid away as the *Chesapeake* sailed toward the open sea.

Commodore Barron was a happy man this lovely morning. He had recently been given command of a squadron of warships. His orders were to hunt the Barbary Pirates, who had been attacking American ships in the far-off Mediterranean Sea.

The *Chesapeake* was a frigate—a fast, three-masted sailing warship of medium size. She had just been repaired and rebuilt so that she was almost a new ship.

She still smelled of freshly cut lumber, and it reminded Barron that he and his men had many things to do. Some of the left-over lumber lay about the decks. It would have to be moved. Otherwise, the gunners would have to climb over the lumber to get to their guns! And the cannon themselves were not in position yet. Powder horns had not been filled, nor had the ammunition been brought up out of storage.

Clearing the decks of the *Chesapeake*. Inset shows Commodore James Barron, who was later court-martialled for the incident.

Ordinarily, Barron would have made certain these things were done before putting out to sea. But he had been in a hurry to get on his way. And he knew he had no enemies to worry about until he reached the Mediterranean Sea, thousands of miles away. Since there were no enemies, it did not matter that his ship was not ready for battle. Many of the men in his crew had never been on a warship in their lives. But Barron planned to train them during the weeks it would take to reach the Mediterranean.

Barron looked around the calm blue bay, and suddenly he frowned. His eye fell upon something he did not like:

three English warships. They were at anchor in the bay, probably taking on supplies from Hampton. There was nothing wrong with this. Great Britain and the United States were supposed to be friends now. But ever since the end of the War for American Independence in 1783, the two countries had been quarreling.

Britain was at war with France, and the war was not going very well for the English. Under Napoleon, the great general and emperor, France had conquered most of Europe. Only Britain's navy had prevented her from being invaded by Napoleon's armies as well.

In the war between Britain and France, the United States was "neutral." Instead of taking sides, she tried to be a friend of both countries. But it wasn't easy to remain neutral. Britain and France kept insisting that the United States choose: either be a friend of Great Britain, or of France, but not both.

The English, especially, were making things difficult for the United States. Commodore Barron knew that these very same ships, that were now peacefully buying supplies in an American town, might fire on an American ship tomorrow! The English claimed the right to stop any ship they believed to be heading toward France and examine the cargo. If the English captain thought the cargo would help the French, he took it. And if the Americans tried to stop him, he might sink their ship.

To Commodore Barron, as to many Americans, this was piracy. But the United States had to put up with it—or else go to war. And the United States was no match for mighty Britain in 1807. Britain's powerful navy controlled the oceans of the whole world.

Even worse than the "piracy" of the English was what they called "impressment." Sometimes the British warships not only stole American cargos, they stole American sailors!

The English claimed that these men were really Englishmen who had run away from English warships. Sometimes this was true. Life was hard on an English warship. And the pay was less than on American warships. Sometimes men did run away. Later they joined an American ship, where they were treated better, and where they weren't likely to be killed by a French cannonball.

The runaway problem was serious for Great Britain. If hundreds of her sailors kept running away to join American ships, how could she defend herself against Napoleon's armies? So British warships stopped American merchant ships and examined their crews. If the British found any sailors they believed to be Englishmen, they took the men off in chains, and sometimes shot them.

Many times these sailors *were* English deserters. But sometimes they were not. Sometimes they were native-born Americans. And sometimes they were Englishmen who had become American citizens. However, the British refused to recognize any English-born American citizens. British law said that any man born an Englishman remained an Englishman till he died. Of course, the government of the United States did not agree with this law. So the two countries quarreled. But Britain paid no attention to American complaints.

This was why Commodore Barron frowned at the English warships. It seemed to him that the English treated the United States as though she were still an English colony, and he didn't like it. Of course, he did not have to worry about his own ship. The *Chesapeake* was not owned by some merchant in Boston or New York. It was a ship of war, owned by the government of the United States. If the English fired on an American warship, that would amount to an act of war.

Barron was a little surprised, however, when the *Chesapeake* reached the open sea. One of the English warships had lifted anchor and followed her out of the bay. The *Leopard* was an English frigate of about the same size as Barron's ship. He knew that the *Leopard* had arrived in Chesapeake Bay only the day before.

By mid-afternoon, the *Chesapeake* was about ten miles off shore. The *Leopard,* sailing right behind, signaled that she was carrying a message for Commodore Barron. Barron let the *Leopard* pull alongside. Several officers crossed over to the *Chesapeake* on a small boat.

A young lieutenant politely handed Barron the message. When the Commodore read it, he could hardly believe his eyes. He had expected a message from his own government, perhaps concerning the Barbary Pirates. Instead, this was a message from the English government. It declared that the *Chesapeake* was to be searched by any English warship that found her. Certain men in the *Chesapeake's* crew were runaways, and they were to be taken off.

Barron thought fast. He was in a dangerous position.

Neither his ship nor his crew was ready to fight. On the other hand, a glance at the *Leopard* told him that the English crew were standing at battle stations. The torches to light the cannon were in their hands! What was he to do? As far as he knew, he had no runaways in his crew.

Barron began to write a reply: English captains do not issue orders to American warships. He handed his answer to the lieutenant, and the officer returned to his ship. While he was being rowed back, Barron ordered his own crew to prepare for battle. But *quietly* — he hoped the English wouldn't notice.

A few minutes later, Barron heard a voice shouting from the *Leopard:* "You understand that I have no choice but to carry out my orders."

Barron stood on the upper deck of his ship. He could see the English sailors standing at their battle stations, waiting. Meanwhile his own crew was running around, trying to do everything at once. He shouted back: "I do not hear what you say!"

A long minute passed. Again Barron heard the voice from the English ship: "You must understand that I have no choice but to carry out my orders!" And again Barron replied, "I do not hear what you say!"

After another minute, the *Leopard* fired a single cannon shot across the bow of the *Chesapeake*. There was a minute's pause, then another shot. Finally, after a brief silence, the *Leopard* roared! All her cannons opened fire on the *Cheasapeake* at once.

In an instant, the masts of the *Chesapeake* were down,

The *Chesapeake* is attacked by the *Leopard*.

the decks were in splinters. Fire and smoke were everywhere, and dead and wounded sailors lay about on all sides. How much Barron wanted to return the fire! But he could not; his guns were not ready. All he could do was urge his men to hurry, to get at least one cannon ready so the *Chesapeake* could get off a single shot.

The English reloaded quickly and fired again. This time Commander Barron himself was wounded. By now, the *Cheasapeake* was a smoldering wreck. Barron had to surrender. He had no choice. He ordered the flag pulled down.

The *Leopard* sent armed men aboard the *Chesapeake*.

13

They examined the American crew and took four sailors away in chains. When Barron tried to surrender his ship, the English officer refused. He could not accept Barron's surrender, he said, because Great Britain and the United States were not at war! So the *Leopard* sailed away.

Barron and what was left of his crew sailed back to Hampton in the crippled ship. What a sad sight it was. The *Chesapeake* had sailed out so proudly in the morning. And now a smoking ruin limped back in.

Commodore Barron was amazed and shocked. Did this mean war, he wondered? Surely the United States could not allow her warships to be attacked on the high seas without going to war?

When news of the attack on the *Chesapeake* reached the people of the United States, they were as shocked as Barron. The cry went up for war. But others asked—how could the United States hope to win a war with Britain? The British had the world's most powerful navy, and one of the most powerful armies. The United States had a tiny navy and hardly any army at all. And what army she had was needed to defend the frontier against Indians.

The country was soon divided on the question. Some favored war, others opposed it. Those who wanted war said that "honor" and the continued independence of the United States were at stake. Those against the war said that the United States could not survive a war with Britain. How would a handful of American warships defend the whole American coast? Not only the cities of the Atlantic coast—Boston, New York, Baltimore, Washington—but far away New Orleans, too!

The answer to this question was that the small American navy simply could not defend the Atlantic coast, much less New Orleans. Yet New Orleans was perhaps the most important of all. It was the key to the huge Louisiana Territory, which the United States had bought from France in 1803. The territory was half of the land owned by the United States!

CHAPTER 2

A Second War For Independence?

The United States did not have to face the difficulty of defending her cities, including New Orleans, for five years. That was how much time passed between the attack on the *Chesapeake* and the beginning of the War of 1812. During those years, Americans argued and argued about whether the United States should go to war. But one man more than any other kept the country out of war, and that was President Thomas Jefferson.

Jefferson had many reasons for wishing to avoid war with Britain. He knew that the American navy and army were no match for the English. But he also believed that war would be bad for the United States. In wartime, men have to give up some of their freedom so that they can all stand together against the enemy. Jefferson valued freedom above everything. He did not think Americans would ever agree about fighting the English.

However, Jefferson did demand that the English apologize. The attack on the *Chesapeake* was against the laws of the sea. But the English government did not really apologize. Their officials admitted the attack had been a mistake. But it never would have happened, they said, if Americans had not tempted English sailors away from their ships.

Jefferson tried to fight back by stopping trade between the United States and Britain. This did hurt the English merchants—but it hurt the American shipping industry as well! Jefferson's enemies said that he was ruining the United States by his policies.

Representatives of the two countries met and talked about the disagreements. The talks got nowhere. The United States wanted the English to stop sinking American ships and impressing American sailors. The English refused. She was at war with France, they said. She could not afford to have American ships trading with France. If France was to be defeated, all trade with that country must be stopped. This would keep her from getting war supplies from other countries. Neither could the English afford to have her sailors running away to American ships.

The English made demands, too. Britain must be allowed to examine—and *tax*—all goods shipped to Europe in American ships! In this way, France's allies in Europe could be kept from trading with the United States, too.

This claim of the right to tax American goods shipped across the Atlantic made Americans even madder. Wasn't Britain trying to make the United States into a colony again? The British had such a powerful navy, some Americans said, she thought she could do whatever she wanted. Well, the United States had won her independence from Britain once. If necessary, she could do it again!

Other Americans, especially those who lived in the New England states, were sympathetic with England. They agreed with much of what the English said. Britain was fighting the

17

tyrant Napoleon, and the United States should help. If the United States had to go to war, they said, it should be with France. After all, they pointed out, the French sometimes sank American ships headed for Great Britain.

Although the New Englanders did not want to fight the British, the farmers along the western frontier strongly favored such a war.

During these years, the "West" meant anything beyond the Appalachian Mountains. At the time of the War for American Independence, the land beyond the mountains had been a wilderness. But by 1812, restless Americans had begun to cross the mountains in greater numbers. Kentucky, Tennessee and Ohio had become states. Many people there wanted war. They knew that the British still held many forts, and controlled areas that belonged to the United States. The westerners believed that the British were encouraging their Indian allies to attack American settlers.

Some Indian tribes along the western frontier were friends of the English. The English gave the Indians advice —and guns. Sometimes the guns were used against American settlers, and this angered the Americans. In the years after 1807, there was more trouble than usual with the Indians.

Actually, many Indians were angry, too—with the Americans. Every year, they saw more and more Americans cross the mountains to take their lands. The Americans paid little attention to whether or not the land they settled had been promised to the Indians by treaty. When the Indians complained to the American government, the government always took the side of the settlers.

In 1810, Indians led by their great chief Tecumseh, began a war of their own against the American settlers. The English gave them guns. A year later, these Indians were defeated at the Battle of Tippecanoe, in Indiana Territory. But they were ready to keep fighting. The Americans were angrier than ever. They blamed the English for the Indian wars, and wanted to go to war with Great Britain. Invade the British colony of Canada, they said, and drive the English out of North America.

Britain still had her hands full, fighting Napoleon, so she hoped to avoid war with the United States. But the English would not give an inch in answer to the American demands.

Some of the men in the English government hoped the Americans *would* declare war. War would give Britain a chance to put the Americans in their proper place. The United States kept growing and growing. One day, she might be a real threat to Canada. Wouldn't it be better if the British put a stop to this growing *now?* The way to stop the growth of the United States was to capture New Orleans.

As far as the English were concerned, they were not certain that the United States owned either New Orleans or the Louisiana Territory. When President Jefferson bought them from France in 1803, England had objected. The English claimed that France had taken Louisiana away from Spain by force. So the real owner was still Spain!

If the Americans declared war, the English would try to capture New Orleans. If they could take the city, the United States would lose control of the Mississippi River. And so the western growth of the United States would be halted.

In 1809, a new president followed Jefferson into the White House in Washington. James Madison was a friend of Jefferson, and a fellow-Virginian. He agreed with Jefferson that the United States should not go to war with Great Britain, but he was not as determined. He did not want Britain to think she could bully the United States.

In 1812, Madison decided that the English did not really want to settle any of their disagreements with the United States. He believed they would continue to make more demands until they had reduced the United States to a colony again. So he asked Congress to declare war on Great Britain, and Congress quickly agreed.

Unfortunately, in 1812 the United States was no more prepared for war than she had been in 1807. Almost nothing had been done to strengthen the army or the navy. And the people were as divided as ever. In New England, they called it "Mr. Madison's War" and said they would not co-operate. Others said it was the Second War for American Independence.

CHAPTER 3

The Fortunes of War

The Americans who favored the war with Britain were called the "War Hawks." They believed that the British were too busy with Napoleon to be able to fight the United States. They wanted to invade Canada immediately.

But the regular army was too small to do it alone. Help would have to come from the militia, the part-time soldiers organized in each state. However, the governors of the New England states, which bordered Canada, refused to call up their militia. The United States government asked for volunteers, but not many men were willing to risk their lives.

The American generals were not very experienced. They could not make up their minds what to do, and they could not agree with each other. They decided to invade Canada from each end of Lake Erie. But the invasion failed.

Now, the Americans had to worry about an invasion *from* Canada. The English won battles at Fort Detroit, Niagara, New York, in Ohio, and in the Michigan Territory. The Great Lakes were almost completely in their hands. And so was the whole northwestern frontier. The Indians began to attack American settlements, and the settlers were forced to retreat toward the mountains.

The situation would have been hopeless for the United States, if it had not been for her small navy. American ships were of the latest design, and far superior to many British warships. Both at sea and on the lakes, the American ships won surprising victories. Americans also proved that, man for man, and ship for ship, their seamanship was as good as the English. But the American navy was never large enough to break the blockade of its large harbors.

More important than the battles at sea, however, were the battles on the lakes. The English had to clear the lakes along the Canadian-American border, if they were going to invade the United States from Canada.

The first of the important lake battles was fought in 1813 on Lake Erie. All that summer, an American shipbuilder named Noah Brown had been directing a crew of men building ships. By September, the Americans were able to put a squadron of ships on the lake that was superior to the English force. Under Master Commandant Oliver Hazard Perry, the Americans attacked on September 15. Their ships had heavier guns, and they soon pounded the English ships into the water.

Perry summed up his victory in a letter to General William Henry Harrison: "We have met the enemy, and they are ours."

When Harrison received Perry's message, he moved quickly. He marched an army of volunteers from Kentucky and Tennessee around Lake Erie and into Canada. A smaller force of Indians and English retreated before him— but not quickly enough. In a battle on the Thames River

Building ships to fight the English.

in Canada, the English-Indian force was destroyed, and Chief Tecumseh was killed.

In April of 1814, bad news came from Europe: Napoleon had surrendered! Now Britain was free to turn all her military power against the Americans. She immediately shipped an army of 10,000 experienced soldiers across the Atlantic to Canada.

The struggle with Napoleon had forced Great Britain to put off any major actions against the United States. From 1812 to April of 1814, the British war aims were simple: to prevent an American invasion of Canada and to blockade

the American ports on the Atlantic. And Britain had been successful. Now she was free to punish the upstart Americans for declaring war on mighty Great Britain.

The English planned a double invasion of the United States. One force would sweep down from Canada through eastern New York. Another, with strong naval support, would capture New Orleans and take control of the Mississippi Valley! And just to keep the Americans off balance, the British navy would raid American cities along the Atlantic coast.

In Canada, 27,000 British troops were ready to invade

the United States. To oppose them, the Americans had only about 7,000 troops. But along the route the English planned to take Lake Champlain. And on the lake was more of the pesky American navy!

Once again, Noah Brown had been busy building ships. This time the English tried to match him at the northern end of Lake Champlain. In September, four English warships and twelve gunboats sailed down the lake in search of four American warships and ten gunboats. The Americans, under the command of Master Commandant Thomas Macdonough, were at anchor near Plattsburg, New York. Macdonough had chosen his position carefully. Although he had fewer boats, his short range guns were heavier. He wanted the fighting to be in close.

As a light wind blew, the ships and boats moved slowly together and began to blast away at each other. When the cannon on one side of Macdonough's flagship, the *Saratoga*, were knocked out, his crew pulled on the anchor ropes to swing the ship around so the other side faced the English. Now the Americans had a fresh battery of guns and they blasted away.

During the fighting, the English commander, Captain George Downie, was killed, and Macdonough was knocked unconscious twice. But when the smoke finally cleared, the Americans had won. All the English warships had been destroyed or captured. Only a few of the gunboats managed to escape.

The American victory at Plattsburg was extremely important. General Sir George Prevost was waiting nearby with an English army, ready to march on New York City. But he did not want to leave the American force on Lake Champlain behind him. So he called off the invasion. He turned back toward Canada to wait for more troops and further orders from England.

For the English, everything now depended upon the capture of New Orleans. If that city could be taken, then the invasion from Canada would not be needed. Ships began to sail southward from Canada, and from along the Atlantic coast of the United States. The plan was for all the ships to gather in the West Indies, off the island of Jamaica, another English colony. From Jamaica, they would all sail together to attack New Orleans.

In the meantime, the English ships raided the American coast, as planned. They entered Chesapeake Bay, from where Commodore Barron had set forth in 1807. The whole bay was defended by only a few gunboats. An army of 4,500 English redcoats, veterans of the war against France, were put ashore. They marched swiftly toward Washington, the new capital of the United States.

The American government was caught by surprise. There were no forts to help defend Washington, and very few troops. A few regular army troops, and some militia from nearby Maryland were hastily given guns and rushed to meet the English. Sailors from the gunboats were also armed and sent to help.

The American and English forces met at Bladensburg, Maryland, a few miles from Washington. But there was hardly a battle. Almost at the first shot, the men in the militia began to run away. This threw other soldiers into a panic, and they began to run too. Only the sailors from the gunboats held their ground and tried to make a fight of it. The Americans had run away so quickly that the "battle" was afterwards called "the Bladensburg Races"!

President Madison and his wife Dolley were eating supper when news of the disaster at Bladensburg reached them. First Mrs. Madison, and then the President, took a boat across the Potomac River, and carriages to the west. They barely escaped in time. When the English commanders, Rear Admiral Sir George Cockburn and Major General Robert Ross, arrived at the White House, they found the food still warm on the table. They sat down and ate it. Then they set fire to the White House, the capitol building, and other public buildings.

Next the English attacked Baltimore, Maryland. Unlike Washington, Baltimore was defended by two forts. When the English troops tried to attack the city, the cannon in the forts drove them away. The English decided to destroy the largest fort, Fort McHenry. To do this, they sailed warships into the wide mouth of the Patapsco River and anchored them just below the fort. Then they began shelling the fort with rockets and burning-hot cannonballs.

Aboard one of the British ships was Francis Scott Key, an American lawyer, who was trying to arrange an exchange of prisoners. All night long he watched the rockets falling on Fort McHenry. It seemed impossible that the fort could hold out. But as the sun rose the next morning, he saw that

The English set Washington to the torch.

the American flag was still flying above the fort. He wished to express his feelings about the event, so he wrote a poem. The poem was later put to music and became our National Anthem—"The Star Spangled Banner."

The British, discouraged, gave up on Baltimore. They had a more important task ahead of them. They loaded their troops back onto their ships and sailed out of Chesapeake Bay. They sailed south, toward Jamaica—and New Orleans.

CHAPTER 4

New Orleans—
The Paris of the New World

In 1814, New Orleans was barely an American city. The United States had owned it only eleven years, since the purchase of the Louisiana Territory from France in 1803. Before that, the city had belonged to either France or Spain for almost one hundred years.

New Orleans was quite unlike any other city in the United States. Some people called it "The Paris of the New World" because it was like the capital of France. Others called it "Queen of the River," because it controlled the mighty Mississippi River.

Most of the people in the city were "Creoles" who were Spanish or French by birth and language. After the Louisiana Purchase, Americans from other parts of the United States had begun to move to the city, but in 1814 they were still only a small part of the population. The Creoles still looked upon them as strangers, *les Américains,* the Americans. The Creoles thought of New Orleans as their city, and they were proud of it.

Because New Orleans was so near the warm waters of the Gulf of Mexico, it was very hot in summer. And because it was surrounded by swamps and marshes, it was also damp. In fact, in summer the city was most like a town on some tropical island in the Caribbean Sea. Flowers were everywhere, and the air was heavy with the scent of azaleas and magnolia. Most of the homes were built with a patio in the middle. Here the Creoles sat on hot afternoons, in the shade of small palm trees, and sipped cool drinks.

The buildings were mainly Spanish and French in style. The windows had large double shutters that could be closed to keep the sun out during the day, and opened to let the breezes in at night. Most of the buildings had small balconies with railings made of beautifully twisted and shaped wrought iron. Leaning on these railings, the Creoles could watch the hubub of the streets from the safety of their homes.

These streets were filled with people chattering to each other in French, Spanish, and English. Just before the War of 1812, the city's population had been greatly increased by the arrival of many people from Santo Domingo and other islands in the Caribbean Sea. Some of them were Negro slaves. Other black people, recently arrived from Africa, added their bright costumes and languages to the color and noise of the street.

Another group of people in the city were the *gens de couleur,* or "people of color." In New Orleans, they were considered different from the white Creoles and from the Negro slaves. The *gens de couleur* might have skin of almost any shade, from very light to dark. But at least one parent, grandparent, or even great-grandparent, was a Negro. And they were not slaves. They were as free as any other citizen of the city. Indeed, the *gens de couleur* were often quite wealthy, and many had Negro slaves of their own. Like the Creoles, they spoke Spanish or French. Also like the Creoles, some had gone to Paris to be educated.

New Orleans was important to the United States even before President Jefferson made the Louisiana Purchase. In 1802, when the city had been returned to the French, Jefferson wrote: "There is on the globe one single spot, the possessor of which is our natural and habitual enemy. It is New Orleans, through which three-eighths of the produce of our territories must pass to market."

In the eleven years since the Louisiana Purchase, New Orleans had become even more important. It was the second greatest port in the country, after New York.

The whole city was built so that it faced the Mississippi River, where ships from all over the world loaded cotton, sugar, leather, furs, and tobacco, or unloaded furniture and fine fabrics from Europe, or slaves from Africa. Alongside the graceful, tall-masted sailing ships were the flat barges, or riverboats.

Farmers and trappers from the Mississippi-Ohio valley came by riverboat to New Orleans. These were the days before the steamship was in use, so the riverboats had to be pushed downriver with the current, using long poles. Once they reached New Orleans, the boats were sold along with their cargoes, since they could not be pushed back upriver against the current. The men who poled the boats had to make their way back home on foot.

The New Orleans docks were busy all day long. Adding to the liveliness were the riverboatmen themselves. When their work was done, they frequently got drunk and sang and shouted—or fought—all night. This often disturbed the citizens of the city, who called these rough and rowdy frontiersmen "Kaintucks," as though they all came from Kentucky.

The center of New Orleans life was the main square, the *Place d'Armes*, which was right beside the river. The Creole ladies and gentlemen could take a leisurely walk around the square and never be out of the sight of the busy activity that brought them their wealth. And, if they chose, they could walk over to the open-air market beside the docks, and select from goods brought from the whole Mississippi-Ohio valley, or from other parts of the world.

The Mississippi River, with its main tributary the Missouri, is the third longest river in the world. In 1814, it was the back door to the United States. It was also the door through which the United States might spread westward across North America. No wonder, then, that the British wanted to take it away!

The English hoped that the New Orleans Creoles would not be loyal to the United States. English spies brought leaflets to the city and secretly tacked them up at street corners. Britain had no quarrel with New Orleans, nor with the Creoles, the leaflets said, only with the Americans. The leaflets promised that if Great Britain gained possession of New Orleans, she would give the city to Spain.

The Creoles read the leaflets with great interest. Most of them had not made up their minds whether they were happy that New Orleans was now an American city or not. The river trade was certainly

KAINTUCK

CREOLES

good business. But these *Kaintucks*—they were not very pleasant people!

The New Orleans Creoles

RIVERBOATMAN

considered themselves elegant ladies and gentlemen. They loved delicately seasoned food, fine wines, beautiful manners, and clothes cut according to the latest fashions in France. When a Creole gentleman had a serious disagreement, he settled it by fighting a duel with swords. So these Kaintucks horrified them. The Kaintucks wore dirty clothes, made out of rough, homespun cloth. They seldom if ever bathed. They could hardly speak without swearing, and most of them could not read or write. And when they fought, they went after each other like animals, with knives and bare hands.

If these particular Americans were examples of what the United States had to offer New Orleans, the Creoles wanted no part of it. So they decided to take a "wait and see" attitude. If the United States defended the city, fine. But they would not fight the English alone.

The governor of Louisiana was an American, William C. Claiborne. He was in charge of the defense of the city, and the English leaflets worried him. Would the citizens of New Orleans remain loyal to the United States?

In September of 1814, Claiborne received a letter that made him even more fearful. It was from Monsieur Jean Lafitte. Lafitte was perhaps the most well-known man in New Orleans, and he was widely respected. He was also a pirate and a smuggler. From his hideout on Barataria Bay, south of the city, Lafitte sent ships and men into the Gulf of Mexico. They captured merchant ships, mostly Spanish, filled with expensive goods. The goods were then brought to New Orleans and sold.

Lafitte was French by birth. He had been in both the English and French navies, and had served as a gunner under Napoleon. But he wasn't satisfied with the strict life and the low pay in the navy, so he became a pirate. Within a few years, he became famous all along the Gulf coast, and in the West Indies.

Claiborne did not like the idea that a pirate — a criminal—was such a prominent citizen. He had tried to arrest him, but succeeded only in capturing his brother, Pierre Lafitte. Claiborne then offered a reward for the capture of Jean Lafitte. But Lafitte replied by offering a much larger reward for the capture of Governor Claiborne! The Creoles thought this was an excellent joke, but Claiborne didn't laugh.

Lafitte's letter surprised Claiborne. Lafitte wrote that he had recently been visited at Barataria by several English naval officers. They requested his aid in capturing New Orleans. Lafitte knew the countryside around New Orleans better than any man alive. It was largely impassable swamp. The English wanted him to show them the best way to approach New Orleans with ships and troops. If he helped them, he would be made a captain in the English navy. His men, and his property would be safe. If he did *not* help, Britain would consider him and his men enemies.

Lafitte described how he had given the English officers a fine dinner, with the best French wines and West Indies cigars. He had politely asked them for fifteen days to think over their offer. The English had agreed. Now he was writing to Claiborne to offer his help to the Americans. He would not, under any circumstances, help the English. In this hour of danger, he wanted to help his new country.

Claiborne did not know what to think. He did not trust Lafitte. But he knew how valuable the pirate could be to the English. And Lafitte had influence among the New Orleans Creoles. Claiborne wrote an urgent letter to the American general in charge of defending New Orleans, General Andrew Jackson, asking him what to do.

Jackson was a hundred miles farther east on the coast of the Gulf of Mexico, helping defend the town of Mobile from an attack by a few English ships. But he replied to Claiborne quickly. He would have nothing to do with any "hellish bandits," he said. He ordered Claiborne to send American troops to Barataria to burn the pirates' hideout to the ground.

Andrew Jackson was a man of strong character and iron will. He was also one of the few successful generals the United States had. President Madison had put him in charge of all the American forces in the South because Jackson had defeated the Creek Indians. The English had

JACKSON   LAFITTE   CLAIBORNE

told the Creeks to attack American settlements in the South, just as Tecumseh and his braves had done farther north.

Jackson led a ragged army of frontiersmen from Kentucky and Tennessee. He was joined by the friendly Cherokee and Choctaw Indians. Together, they fought the Creeks for months. Finally, he destroyed them in the Battle of Horseshoe Bend, on the Tallapoosa River, in what is now Alabama.

Jackson was born and raised on the frontier, fighting Indians much of the time. From his birth place in northern

South Carolina, he moved west as the frontier moved west, settling in Tennessee. He became a farmer, a lawyer, and finally a Congressman from Tennessee. Jackson could be easily angered, and because of this he took part in many duels.

One of his most famous duels was fought with Charles Dickinson, who was known as the best shot on the whole frontier. Most people were sure Jackson would be killed. The two men met at dawn and walked the required number of steps from each other. At the signal, Dickinson snapped off a shot instantly. But Jackson still stood.

"My God!" Dickinson exclaimed, "have I missed him?"

Jackson took careful aim and pulled the trigger. The gun didn't fire. He cocked it, aimed again, and pulled the trigger once more. This time the gun fired, and Dickinson fell to the ground dead. Jackson slowly walked to a waiting carriage and rode away. Only in the carriage did he admit that he had been hit—in the chest. His boots were filled with blood.

"I'd have hit him," Jackson remarked, "even if he had shot me through the brain."

Jackson planned to defend New Orleans with the same determination. He believed his country's honor was at stake. And he hated the English. During the War for Independence, when he was still a child, an English officer had struck him with a sword because he refused to polish the officer's boots. Jackson still bore the scar, and the grudge.

In late November, Jackson marched toward New

Orleans at the head of his small army, including a thousand Choctaw braves, led by their great chief, Pushmataha. Heavy rains turned the road into deep mud. Jackson was very ill. Still he pushed on, marching with his men, and like them sleeping on the cold damp ground.

On December 1, he arrived at New Orleans. The sight of this man on a mud-splattered horse, his clothes soaked with rain, was hardly inspiring to the people of New Orleans. He wore an old coat, a battered hat, his boots were down at the heel and crusty with mud, and his face was gray with sickness. The word spread quickly throughout the city: *Le Général* Jackson was nothing but an old Kaintuck!

CHAPTER 5

The Armada

Jackson immediately set up headquarters in the heart of the city, and began planning its defenses. But he soon learned that he had his hands full with the New Orleans Creoles. They did not seem very anxious to defend their city against the British. He wrote to his beloved wife, Rachel, about his difficulties. He also begged her to visit him at New Orleans; he had not seen her for many months.

Of course, Jackson was not the only one making plans for New Orleans. Two thousand miles across the Gulf of Mexico, on the island of Jamaica, the British were making plans of their own for the Paris of the New World.

Throughout October and early November, the skies over Jamaica were clear. The pale green waters of Negril Bay lay calm and peaceful as the palms along the shore nodded in the light breezes. But the bay itself bristled with the masts of ships, like an angry porcupine! These were not the usual merchant ships, loaded with Jamaican rum or sugar. One and all, they were warships, full of guns and troops.

Never before had such a powerful naval force been gathered in one place in the New World. There were more than fifty ships crowded into the small bay. The British were determined to capture New Orleans, and they were taking no chances. With this giant armada, they believed they could easily deliver the death-blow to American hopes in the War of 1812.

The British now considered the capture of New Orleans the most important thing they could accomplish in this war. For if they captured New Orleans, they did not mean to give it back—ever.

The ships in Negril Bay were ready to go. Bobbing up and down in the water, they seemed to pull at their anchors. Below deck on the flagship, the *Tonnant,* the English commanders planned their attack. Standing around a large table, they studied a map showing the coastline very clearly and in detail. But beyond the shores, it provided very little information. The officers knew that New Orleans was surrounded by thick swamps full of alligators and other wild beasts. But where were the swamps, and how could they be crossed? This map could not tell them.

While the officers planned below, above decks there were some very surprising passengers on the largest of the ships. Elegant English ladies walked about, talked among themselves, and from time to time their laughter rang out across the beautiful bay. They were the wives of the officers, and they too planned to visit New Orleans. With such a mighty armada, the capture of the city could not take very long. Then they would all put on their best gowns and take a slow walk around the Place d'Armes!

Below deck on the *Tonnant,* the officers at last decided on a plan of action. According to the map, there were two large bodies of water near New Orleans—Lake Pontchartrain and Lake Borgne. Although they were called lakes, they actually could be reached by ship from the Gulf of Mexico. The armada would sail into Lake Borgne, since it was closer, and put men ashore. The lake was 40 miles east of New Orleans. The men could explore the area until they found the best way to approach the city.

Soon a single cry was heard from one end of Negril Bay to the other: "Lift anchors! We're off to New Orleans!" All at once, the pale green bay turned white with the unfurling sails. In a few hours it was empty, as the fifty English ships hurried toward the shore of Louisiana.

The English left Jamaica just as Jackson began his march to New Orleans. Like the Americans, they ran into bad weather. In fact, they sailed right into a hurricane. The ships were scattered, and many were damaged. It was weeks before they all managed to regather and move once again toward New Orleans.

In New Orleans, Jackson began to rally the support of the Creoles. Their first opinion of him changed. They began to admire him. He put on a fancy dress uniform with a cream-colored coat, new boots, and a new hat. It turned out that Andy Jackson was rather a handsome man. He was tall and thin and held himself very straight at all times. He had a high forehead and piercing eyes that charmed the ladies and frightened most men. He soon told them all exactly what he planned to do.

"We will drive the enemy into the sea, or die in the attempt!" The people cheered. Everyone felt the city was in strong and able hands.

One of the leading citizens of New Orleans was an old acquaintance of Jackson's named Edward Livingston. Livingston had been a Congressman at the same time as Jackson, and they had shared the same opinions on many issues. Livingston was now the attorney for Jean Lafitte. He told the general that Lafitte would be very valuable in planning the defense of New Orleans, and offered to arrange a meeting. Claiborne had destroyed his hideout in Barataria, but Lafitte still wanted to help, Livingston said.

Jackson refused. He set about trying to defend the city in his own way. But he found that no one seemed to be able to give him a very clear picture of the countryside around New Orleans. And his maps were poor.

Jackson had two warships with which to defend the city, the *Carolina* and the *Louisiana*. This wasn't much, but even they could not be used, because they didn't have enough men to sail them or to handle the cannon. When Jackson asked the Louisiana legislature to draft men to work on the ships, the legislature replied: Ask for help from Lafitte.

Finally Jackson gave in. He agreed to let Livingston arrange a meeting. Once he met the pirate, Jackson was won over. He asked Lafitte what he wanted in return for his help. Lafitte said he asked for nothing at all. But he *hoped* his country would look with favor upon his actions. Jackson promised to try and get him a pardon from the American government.

Jackson made Lafitte one of his top assistants. Lafitte's

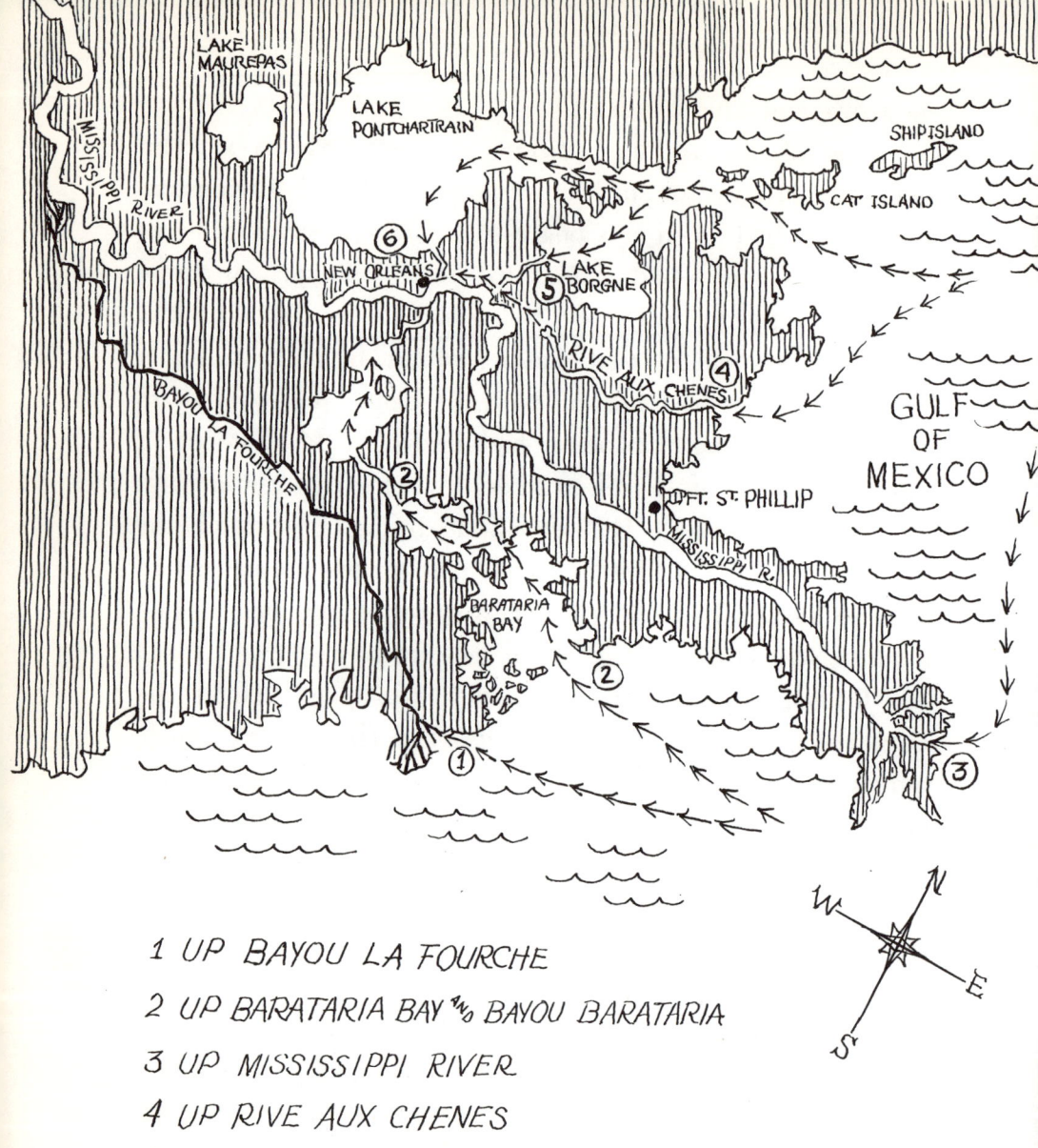

1 UP BAYOU LA FOURCHE
2 UP BARATARIA BAY AND BAYOU BARATARIA
3 UP MISSISSIPPI RIVER
4 UP RIVE AUX CHENES
5 INTO LAKE BORGNE (ROUTE TAKEN)
6 INTO LAKE PONTCHARTRAIN AND BAYOU ST. JOHN

Pirate Lafitte's map of the six approaches to New Orleans.

men were added to the defenders, both on the ships and ashore. Lafitte's gunners were famous for their skill. He showed Jackson the six ways the English could approach New Orleans, and told him how to defend against each. And he drew exact maps.

In the meantime, another problem had come up. The people of the city wanted to know what Jackson planned to do about the *gens de couleur*. Would he let them defend the city—with guns?

From the earliest days, the *gens de couleur* in New Orleans had always had their own militia units. In recent years, as more and more *gens de couleur* from Santo Domingo had been arriving in the city, they had formed a militia unit, too. But some of the white New Orleanians were afraid to let any of them have guns. They were afraid they would use them to free their Negro brothers and sisters, the slaves.

Livingston and others assured Jackson that these fears were silly. In fact, the *gens de couleur* were probably among the city's most loyal defenders. Besides, if Jackson refused to let them defend the city, he would insult them. Then they might go over to the English. Jackson ordered the Negro units armed, and welcomed them as American citizens and fellow-defenders.

When the paymaster for the troops was unwilling to pay the *gens de couleur*—as well as the Choctaws—Jackson sent him an angry note:

"It is enough for you to receive my orders for the payment of troops, without asking whether they are white, black, or tea!"

CHAPTER 6

The First Battle

The English ships arrived off the Louisiana coast on December 10. They dropped anchor near Ship and Cat islands, not far from the entrance to Lake Borgne. The islands were uninhabited, but the English ships were spotted immediately. Jackson had put five small gunboats, under Lieutenant Thomas Ap Catesby Jones, on Lake Borgne. The men on these boats saw the English ships, and word was quickly sent to Jackson.

The English commander, Vice-Admiral Sir Alexander Cochrane, saw the American gunboats, too. He had encountered gunboats like these before from Maine to Maryland. He decided that before he did anything else, he would destroy them. He ordered several medium-sized frigates to chase the gunboats.

Lieutenant Jones knew Lake Borgne well. It was very shallow, with mud only a few feet below the surface in many places. Jones's small boats could sail over these shallow places, but the larger frigates could not. Jones let the English ships chase him around the lake, then lured them into the shallows. They ran aground on the mud.

Cochrane saw his mistake. He wouldn't send any more big ships after the Americans—not on Lake Borgne. Instead, he sent a fleet of gunboats and barges loaded with troops and cannons. The barges had to be poled along, but they could move on the shallowest water. After chasing the American gunboats for 37 miles around Lake Borgne, they caught them at last.

Jones's boats were trapped in a small cove. The wind had died, so the boats could not move. Slowly, but surely, the English boats and barges moved in. There were 45 English vessels in all, carrying 1,200 men. Jones had 182 men on his five boats. They couldn't escape. So they decided to stay and fight.

The English moved their barges in until they were right alongside the American boats. Then the troops swarmed onto the American boats. The fighting was fierce,

Hopelessly outnumbered, the Americans are beaten in hand-to-hand fighting.

and it lasted more than two hours. Most of it was hand to hand. Jones was wounded, and one-fourth of his men were either wounded or killed, before the Americans surrendered.

This was the first battle for New Orleans, and the English had won it.

Now Jackson had no boats or ships on either Lake Borgne or Lake Pontchartrain, for he had kept the *Carolina* and the *Louisiana* on the Mississippi River. More important, he had lost his "eyes" on the lakes. He had no one to watch the English and report what they were doing. The English could land troops anywhere on the shore of the two lakes without his knowledge.

As they had planned, the English dropped men off along the shores of Lake Borgne. They began looking for a way to reach New Orleans. They found a number of bayous—small, slow streams threading the swamps. But, following Lafitte's advice, Jackson had blocked them all with logs.

One day, however, English soldiers came across a cluster of palm huts almost hidden among the high marsh grass. A few Spanish and Portuguese fishermen lived in the huts. Every day they sold their catch of fish in New Orleans. But how did they reach New Orleans, the English wanted to know? For a few coins, the fishermen agreed to show them.

For some reason, one of the bayous that emptied into Lake Borgne had not been blocked by logs, as Jackson had ordered. This was the Bayou Bienville, which began in a swamp only eight miles from New Orleans. The fishermen took the English with them as they poled their flat-bottomed boat up the bayou. Then they walked a few hundred yards through a swamp, and they were on the banks of Mississippi River. It was dry land from here to the city. The English soldiers hurried back to tell the others. Within hours, English troops were being paddled and poled up Bayou Bienville.

In New Orleans, no one suspected that the English were almost at the edge of the city. In fact, the people were cheered by the arrival of more American troops. Marching both day and night, some 800 men Jackson had earlier stationed at Baton Rouge covered 135 miles in only three days. Their commander was a lifelong friend of Jackson, General James Coffee. And only a few hours later, three thousand militia arrived on riverboats from Tennessee under General William Carroll. They had left Tennessee a month earlier, and General Carroll used the long journey to train them.

The new arrivals doubled Jackson's forces—he now had about 6,000 men. He was in conference with Carroll and Coffee when three men suddenly burst into the room. One was a young man, breathless and sweating, in stained and torn clothing. He began speaking rapidly and excitedly to Jackson in French. Another of the men stepped forward to translate. This young man was Major Gabriel Villeré of the Louisiana militia, the translator explained. And he claimed to have seen the English troops in large numbers eight miles from the city!

Jackson had been seated on a sofa. Now he sprang to his feet and hammered a nearby table with his fist. "By the Eternal!" he exclaimed. "They shall not sleep on our soil! I'll smash them, so help me God!"

CHAPTER 7

"We Must Fight Them Tonight!"

Villeré quickly told his story. That morning, he had been sitting on the porch of his home, the Villeré plantation, eight miles east of New Orleans. Suddenly, out of the cypress woods came hundreds of soldiers—English soldiers! They surrounded his house and took him prisoner. They asked a lot of questions about the defenses of the city. He told them lies. They asked how many men Jackson had, and he said 12,000. They treated him very courteously because he was a French Creole, and they hoped he would help them. But when they weren't watching him carefully, he slipped away and ran all the way to New Orleans.

Jackson thanked Villeré, and offered him a glass of wine. Then he called for all his officers and told them the situation. A force of English troops was within an hour's march of the city. The size of this force was not known. But it was certainly large enough to make a strong attack against New Orleans at any moment. "Gentlemen," Jackson concluded, "we must fight them tonight!"

Jackson tried not to show it, but for the first time he was alarmed. He had reports that the English might have as many as 20,000 men, more than three times the number of Americans. Not only that, Jackson's forces were scattered over all six routes the English might take to attack the city. The English force at the Villeré plantation might be the main English attack. If so, he would need every man he had. But what if it was only an attempt to draw his troops from one of the other six routes?

In any case, Jackson was certain that he had to do *something* about the redcoats on the Villeré plantation. They had almost caught him by surprise. Well, now he would attack them by surprise! He would hit them before they had a chance to get organized.

Jackson marched immediately with a few hundred soldiers to the east of the city. Behind him he left orders for as many troops as could be collected to follow him. Outside the city, Jackson rode his white horse up onto the high levee (an earthen wall to protect against floods) that

General Jackson atop the levee, checking on the *Carolina*.

ran along the bank of the Mississippi River. It was late in the afternoon. He could barely make out the crew of the *Carolina* as they pulled up anchor and hurried to their battle stations.

Jackson hoped the *Carolina*'s cannons would help make up for his lack of troops. He had ordered the ship to lift anchor, but not to put up sails. It was to drift with the current down toward the English. When it was alongside them, it would quietly drop anchor again and wait. He hoped the English would neither hear nor see it. At exactly 7:30 p.m., the ship would suddenly open fire. That would be the signal for Jackson's attack.

The battle would take place on a field of sugarcane right beside the Mississippi River. The cane had been cut down and there was only a stubble left, so it would be like an open field. On one side there was the levee and the river. On the other was a thick cypress swamp. Cutting across the canefield and running into the swamp were two canals. Jackson stopped at one of these, the Rodríguez canal, and waited for nightfall before moving any farther. Far away across the cane stubble and out of sight was another canal, the Villeré canal, where the English were setting up their headquarters.

By nightfall, Jackson had about a thousand men at the Rodríguez canal. He had no way knowing how many English troops he would be facing. Slowly, and silently, Jackson and his men crept toward the English. They didn't stop until they could hear English voices and see their campfires. Jackson sent a small band of Choctaws and frontiersmen under General Coffee to circle around through the swamp and attack the English from the side. These men could move even through swamp in complete silence, and as invisibly as deer.

The night was misty and cold. But for a change, there was no rain. Occasionally, the moon broke through the patches of mist and cloud to give a ghostly glow to the canefield. Jackson's scouts reported that they guessed the English force to be about a thousand men. For Jackson, this was both good news and bad news. Good because it meant the Americans would not be outnumbered. Bad because it meant that most of the English troops were somewhere else! What if they attacked the city from another direction while he was busy here?

At exactly 7:30, the big cannon on the *Carolina* began to roar, shelling the astonished English. They could not tell at first where the fire was coming from. When they located the ship at last, they rushed a few small cannons to fire back. Just as they did, Jackson's men attacked out of the darkness.

Surprised a second time, the English troops began to fall back. Where had all these men come from? They seemed to appear out of nowhere, like demons. But the English troops were experienced. They soon recovered themselves and began to fight. Before long, they had stopped retreating, and were beginning to push the Americans back.

Then, out of nowhere, a screaming band of wild men and Indians jumped out of the cedar swamp. Again, the amazed English fell back. But by this time, their officers had managed to move up and take charge of the men. They ordered them into formation, turning two groups to face the attack from the swamp. Coffee's men, outnumbered, had to break loose and join the other American troops. A few were captured.

The English made a strong attack near the edge of the swamp. They moved forward so quickly that some of them almost managed to capture several American cannons that had been brought up. But Jackson rode up on a huge white horse, shouting, "Save the guns! Save the guns!" His men rallied and stopped the English attack.

The fighting continued for four hours. In the dark, it was hard to tell friend from enemy. To make matters worse, a thick fog began rolling in from the river. In the gunsmoke, fog, and darkness, men fought mostly hand to hand. For some Americans, this was a good thing. Their old rifles refused to fire—but they made excellent clubs! The Americans were able to keep their sense of direction because of a 14-year-old Negro drummer boy. Jordan Noble kept up a steady rat-tat-tat, as Jackson said later, "in the hottest hell of fire" of the battle.

Finally, just before midnight, both sides fell back, exhausted. The Americans withdrew behind the Rodríguez canal. Each side allowed the other to take its own dead and wounded from the field.

Jackson was satisfied that he done what he wanted to do. He had caught the English off balance. And his crazy-quilt of an army—Creoles, *gens de couleur,* Santo Domingans, pirates, Choctaws and frontiersmen—had fought it out with Europe's finest army, man for man, and had not given an inch.

CHAPTER 8

The English Attack

The Americans brought bales of cotton from the New Orleans wharves and piled them along the canal for protection from the English cannon and musket fire. Then they dug trenches for themselves behind the cotton bales. Overnight, they made a strong defensive line. And they waited.

Jackson's scouts told him that English troops had continued to arrive all during the night of December 23, and through the early morning. At dawn, December 24, the canefield was completely covered by a thick blanket of fog. Jackson expected an attack any moment. The fog would give the English a great advantage. They would be covered until they came within a few yards of the American lines. But the morning passed, and there was no attack.

The scouts reported that English troops were still arriving. As it became clearer that this was going to be the main English attack, Jackson ordered more of his troops to join him at the Rodríguez canal.

As Christmas Eve passed, the troops shivered in their trenches. The cold damp seemed to seep into their bones. They would have liked to celebrate the holiday, but that wasn't possible.

There was little celebration in New Orleans either. It

59

was hard to be joyful when your city, your home, and perhaps your life depended upon the outcome of a battle about to take place eight miles away. A rumor began to spread that Jackson planned to burn New Orleans to the ground if he lost this battle! He didn't want the English to get their hands on all the supplies in the city. People did not known whether to believe this story or not.

On the morning of Christmas Day, the English cannons began to roar. But no cannonballs fell on the American lines, and there was no attack. Jackson's scouts reported that the cannons had been fired to announce the arrival of Sir Edward Pakenham, the supreme commander of all the English forces at New Orleans.

When this news spread among the Americans, there was some feeling of relief. Many of them believed that the Duke of Wellington himself was going to lead the English forces. Wellington, the man who had defeated Napoleon, was considered the greatest general in the world.

Some of the English soldiers had heard that Wellington would lead them, too. And they were disappointed. But Pakenham, who was Wellington's brother-in-law, was an excellent general. He had proven both his skill as a commander and his bravery in fighting the French in Spain. This was the first time the English had sent one of their top generals to lead an attack against the Americans.

Pakenham studied the situation of his troops, and he didn't like what he saw. The American line, dug in behind the canal, was too strong. To attack it, the English would have to march across hundreds of yards of open field. In doing so, they would be perfect targets for American fire. He wanted to load all his men back on the ships and land them somewhere else.

Pakenham's men objected. Retreat? *Never,* they said. Not from these "Dirtyshirts." The English had noted the dirty, homespun clothes of the men they had captured. These men weren't soldiers, they said. Americans couldn't fight. They would panic and run, just as they had at Bladensburg.

Pakenham listened to his men, and he allowed himself to be persuaded. Very well, he said, let the battle be fought here. But he knew that the battle might well be won or lost by artillery. So he ordered more cannons to be brought from the English ships to the battlefield. The first thing he would have to do would be to destroy the *Carolina* and the *Louisiana.*

On the morning of December 27, there was no wind at all. The Americans along the Rodríguez canal felt uneasy. Things were too quiet. Then, suddenly, the roar of cannons broke out from the English lines.

Before the Americans had time to realize what was happening, the English cannons hit the *Carolina.* Under the cover of darkness the previous night, the English had brought cannons up onto the levee, close to the ship. They had heated the cannonballs in their campfires until they were red-hot. When one of them hit the wooden ship, it started a fire.

Within a few minutes, the *Carolina* was in flames, and the fire was moving quickly toward the ammunition. All at once the men began leaping over the sides of the ship into the cold Mississippi. Then there was an explosion that was so loud, it was heard clearly in New Orleans, eight miles away! The *Carolina* was lost.

Now the English cannons turned on the *Louisiana,* which had been floated down beside the *Carolina.* The crew had already leaped into rowboats which were tied with ropes to the bow of the ship. The men would try to row her to safety. With no wind to fill the sails, it was the only way to get the ship out of range.

The American troops climbed the levee to watch—there was nothing they could do to help. They could see the sailors, many of them Jean Lafitte's pirates, straining at the oars as the redhot cannonballs fell around them. Inch by inch, foot by foot, the ship was towed upstream against the current, and away from the English cannons. The cannonballs began to fall short. The *Louisiana* was saved! The men on the bank gave the sailors a loud cheer.

Then they hurried back to their positions to prepare for the English attack. They waited all that day. That night, few of them were able to sleep, for they expected the English to appear out of the darkness—as *they* had—any minute.

Finally, just before dawn on December 28, the long-awaited attack came. The English troops formed neat even lines, about sixty men across. They put bayonets on the ends of their guns. As the soldiers marched towards the waiting Americans, they kept their neat lines, as though they were on parade. A strange, wailing music—the sound

The *Louisiana* is towed out of range of English cannonfire.

of Scottish bagpipes—rose up behind them. For a while nothing could be heard but the sound of the bagpipes, droning like musical cats, and the sucking sound of boots on the soggy canefield.

The American cannons opened fire, from one end of their line to the other. The English soldiers in the first few lines fell forward into the mud. From the deck of the *Louisiana*, which had been pulled back behind the American lines, Master Commandant Daniel Patterson watched the English through a small telescope. When they were in range, he ordered the ship's cannons to open fire. More redcoats fell. The neat lines of the English began to break apart. But the men continued to march on.

Jackson was on his horse, about to hurry to his front lines, when an elegantly dressed man stepped up and called out to him. Jackson pulled in his horse. The man was Bernard Marigny, probably the wealthiest Creole citizen of New Orleans, and a member of the Louisiana legislature. Jackson asked Marigny what he wanted.

As the cannons roared and the cannonballs fell only yards away, Marigny coolly bowed. Would *le général* please explain why he had ordered the Louisiana legislature closed, Marigny asked? Jackson replied: because he had heard that there were members of the legislature who were planning to make peace with the English.

Marigny assured Jackson that the legislature was completely loyal. But there was just one question.

"Yes, what is it? Out with it, man!" Jackson shouted above the noise of the battle.

There was a rumor, Marigny said, that Jackson planned to burn New Orleans to the ground if he lost the battle. The people were naturally concerned for their homes.

When Jackson said nothing, Marigny continued. Would *le général* please say what he planned to do if he lost the battle?

Jackson's eyes almost leaped from his head. "Monsieur Marigny," he growled, "if I thought the hair on my head knew my thoughts on that subject, I would cut it off and *burn* it!"

With that, Jackson wheeled his horse about and rode away. Marigny decided to stay and see who would win the battle.

The American cannons were tearing great holes in the English lines, but the English kept marching. When they came within rifle range, Kentucky and Tennessee "squirrel shooters" were as deadly as the cannons.

On the left side of the American lines, near the swamp, the English made the most progress. They were the farthest distant from the cannons of the *Louisiana*. Coffee had again taken some men into the cedar swamps, but was forced to retreat. Pakenham did not want the men on that side to get too far ahead of the rest of his forces, so he ordered them to halt. While they waited, Jackson sent reinforcements. When the English started forward again, they were driven back.

A bugle was heard above the roar of cannons—the call for retreat! The redcoats formed lines once again, and began marching backward. They continued to face the

Americans, their bayonets glistening in the sunlight. The air was filled with smoke and the cries of English wounded, and the canefield was covered with the red coats of the English dead. The attack had failed.

Marigny returned to New Orleans in a cheerful mood. He had braved the battlefield to speak to the terrifying *général*. And he had seen the Americans drive the English off the field. New Orleans was saved.

At least for one day.

CHAPTER 9

The Great Cannon Duel

For the first night in more than a week, the people of New Orleans were able to sleep a little easier in their beds. But not the English soldiers. They had expected to be in New Orleans already. Instead they were back in their tents, in the cold and damp. From time to time, the Americans sent a cannonball into their camp to remind them of the defeat they had just suffered.

Next morning Jackson was up at dawn, examining the English lines through a telescope. There were no preparations for another attack. He suspected that they had had enough for awhile, but they would attack again. He decided to use the time making his line even stronger.

Jackson ordered raised wooden platforms built for some of his larger cannons. This would allow the men to aim them better. He also ordered three cannons taken off the *Louisiana*. They were taken back to New Orleans, put on the ferry, then hauled down along the riverbank to a position where they could fire at the English across the river.

During the following mornings, Jackson and his officers were up early, checking the English lines through their telescopes. But the English showed no signs that they were ready to march against the American line. Jackson's scouts, moving near the English camp through the swamp, reported

Raised platforms hold American cannons for better aim.

that the English were bringing many more cannons from their ships.

Pakenham did not admit that his men had been defeated on December 28. In his official report, he wrote that he had only been testing the Americans, to find out their strength and weakness. From this bloody "test" he had learned that the American artillery made their line too strong to attack directly. So he had decided to destroy, or at least reduce, their artillery with artillery of his own.

By New Year's Eve, his men had increased their cannons to 24, of various sizes. The Americans had only 15 cannons, including the three on the opposite side of the river. Now Pakenham was ready.

The morning of New Year's Day, 1815, was foggy, like so many previous mornings. An Englishman later wrote that it was still so dark, late in the morning, that it was as though the day did not want to begin at all. And it was cold, too.

The English troops were put in formation for an attack. But Pakenham did not take advantage of the fog. Instead, he held the men back, and waited. Before he sent any more men across that canefield, he wanted to destroy the American cannons. To do that, his own gunners needed to be able to see their targets. The morning passed slowly, in an uneasy quiet, as both sides waited.

About mid-morning, the fog cleared away, and the English cannons began to fire. The English gunners were well-trained army men. They moved quickly, pushing in the gunpowder, the cannon balls, the packing, and then touching the fuse with their torches. All along the English lines the cannons fired, one after another, like a single machine.

At first, the answering fire seemed slow and weak. The Americans had only a few regular army gunners. Most of their cannons were fired by New Orleans militiamen, sailors from the *Carolina*, or Lafitte's pirates. The Americans worked more slowly. They fired, checked through a spyglass where their balls hit, adjusted the aim of their cannons, and fired again.

As the morning passed, the Americans' aim grew better

KING'S OWN REGIMENT OF FOOT   LT. OF DRAGOONS   HIGHLAND INFANTRY

Uniforms of British troops.

and better. One after another of the English batteries was hit. And with each hit, the Americans fired much more rapidly—more rapidly than the English.

The usual way of protecting a battery of cannons was to pile bags of sand around it. But in the swamps the only sand was quicksand. So instead of sand, the English went to the nearby plantations and got big barrels of raw sugar which they heaped around their batteries. The sugar looked a lot like sand, but it was not as heavy. And it proved useless. Whenever a cannonball hit the barrels of sugar, they exploded into splinters.

As the day wore on, the English gunners grew hot, thirsty and tired. Some of them tried to eat the raw sugar, thinking it would make them feel better. Instead, it made them sick.

One by one, the English cannons stopped firing. Some of the men ran away; others were wounded or killed. Their cannons were blasted to pieces. By one o'clock in the afternoon, every one of the English cannons was silent. But the American cannons were still firing, faster than ever. It was a total defeat for the English artillery.

Pakenham ordered his troops back to their tents. The success of American artillery had put the American army in a better position than before. He knew that once again he would have to send his men into blistering fire. But he was in no hurry to do that. Perhaps with a little time, he would be able to think of a better way.

CHAPTER 10

Field of Diamonds— Field of Blood

Jackson knew that the duel of the cannons had hurt the English. They would have to change their plans. But what would they do? He tried to guess.

The canefield was no longer a good place for the English to attack, he decided. With each day that passed, his men dug in deeper. The advantage lay entirely with the defender on this battlefield. Wouldn't the English try to go around him? With their ships, they could easily move a large number of troops to some other place. He ordered his scouts to keep close watch.

Jackson believed the English were most likely to sail into Lake Pontchartrain and land north of New Orleans. So he sent troops to a position north of the city, and hoped they would be enough.

It was also possible that the English would try to cross the Mississippi River. Then they could march up the opposite side, or west bank. Jackson had only the three cannons on that side, plus a few hundred supporting troops. If the English could get enough men to that side of the river, they might capture the cannons and aim them at the Americans on the east bank of the river!

On January 4, fresh American troops arrived down

the river from Kentucky. But these squirrel shooters had no guns. Jackson could not believe it. "I have never seen a Kentuckian in my life," he said, "without a gun, a pack of cards, and a bottle of whiskey!" Nevertheless, it was true.

Jackson sent some of the men to New Orleans to collect whatever guns might still be left among the people there. Then he ordered about 500 of them to take the ferry across to the west bank to join the men protecting the cannons on that side. But less than half of them had been able to find guns.

In the meantime, Jackson kept his eye on the English. He could see that they were busy about something, but none of his scouts could find out what it was they were doing. The Americans made life miserable for the English troops. Every day some of the Choctaws and frontiersmen sneaked around through the swamp. From their hiding places, they would pick off a soldier with a single shot. Or they might creep up and kill one with their knives! The English were soon terrified of the swamp.

Jackson replaced the cotton bales along the canal with a higher, stronger wall made out of mud. From behind this wall, his men could fire with very little danger of being hit themselves. And for the English to reach the American lines, they would have to march across hundreds of yards of cane stubble, wade the canal, and then climb the slippery mud wall.

On January 6, Jackson learned that the English were building ladders to climb the mud wall. Expecting an attack at dawn, he ordered his men on the alert.

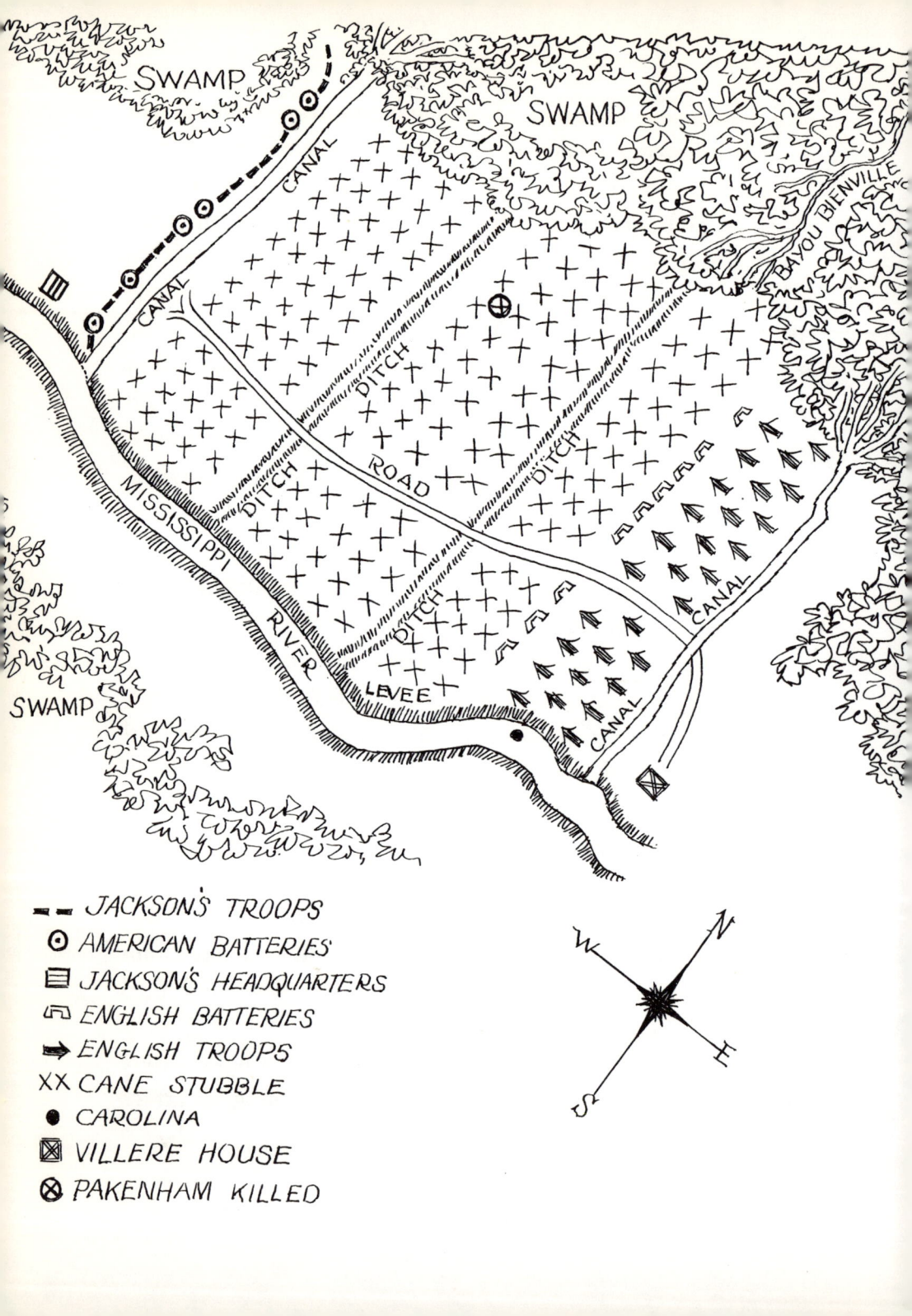

- - JACKSON'S TROOPS
- ⊙ AMERICAN BATTERIES
- ☰ JACKSON'S HEADQUARTERS
- ⌂ ENGLISH BATTERIES
- ➡ ENGLISH TROOPS
- ✕✕ CANE STUBBLE
- • CAROLINA
- ⊠ VILLERE HOUSE
- ⊗ PAKENHAM KILLED

As Jackson had guessed, Pakenham's plan was to cross the Mississippi and move quickly up the river to capture the American batteries on that side. But in order to succeed, he would have to get his men across the Mississippi without the Americans knowing it.

Pakenham's "secret" was that he was digging a canal. Or rather, his men were lengthening the Villeré canal. They were digging from the end of the canal *through* the river levee to the river itself. On the night of January 7, dozens of boats were brought up Bayou Bienville. The last of the canal was dug, and water from the Mississippi flooded into it. But it didn't turn out as Pakenham expected.

He had expected to move the boats easily up the canal to the river, put his men aboard them, and send them across the river. And all this was to be done during the night, so the Americans wouldn't see. But the water from the river rushed into his canal with such force, that it was almost impossible to pull the boats against it!

All night his men pulled the boats to the river. Dawn approached, and still all the boats had not been hauled over. There was no time to waste, so the troops were loaded into what boats were available. They began to row across the river, but again their plans were spoiled. The river was over a mile wide, and did not appear to have much of a current. However, the current was so fast in mid-stream the boats caught in it were swept far downstream. They were miles from where they intended to land.

Dawn broke on January 8—and once again there was

fog. Pakenham waited impatiently for his men. At dawn, the commander of the forces crossing the river, Colonel William Thornton, was supposed to signal that he was ready to attack the American batteries. But no signal came.

Once again, both sides waited for the battle, as the sun tried to break through. Behind their mud wall, the Americans peered into the thick gray fog, expecting to see the redcoats come through it at any moment. Very slowly, the fog began to lift. As it did so, Americans saw an astonishing sight. Tiny drops of water were clinging to the cane stubble. The morning sun, shining through the drops of water, made them gleam and glisten like diamonds. The whole canefield seemed to be shimmering in diamonds!

But suddenly the black boots of the English troops could be seen, trampling the diamonds—and then the red coats. Not wanting to wait until the fog was entirely gone, Pakenham had sent his men forward without a signal from the west bank.

The English troops were again marching in perfect formation across the entire canefield. Pakenham had put the men near the edge of the swamp under General Gibbs. Those between the river and the levee, under General Keane. He hoped his men would be able to break through the American line at one of these points, and then attack the Americans from the rear.

On the swamp side, General Gibbs's men were cut down by American cannon fire. Row after row of redcoats marched toward the Americans, but they were soon stumbling over the heaped bodies of their dead and wounded comrades. When they came in range of the squirrel shooters under General Coffee, even more redcoats fell to the ground. The Americans stood in three lines. First one line would fire. As the men stepped back to reload, another line stepped up to fire. By the time the third line had fired, the first was again ready. Experienced English officers later said they had never faced such rapid and accurate fire in their entire lives.

It became more and more difficult for the English troops to march forward—they couldn't get over the heaps of dead and wounded. But when they tried to run away, they ran into the men marching behind them. General Gibbs tried to get his men to form lines and continue the attack, but he was shot dead. General Pakenham also rode forward, but he was killed by a cannonball.

On the river side, General Keane and his men fared no better. Some of them just managed to reach the canal, only to be shot down and drowned in it. A few actually succeeded in climbing the mud wall. But they too were shot, and fell wounded into the arms of the Americans. Keane himself was badly wounded. Of 700 men, he lost more than 500.

The English soldiers continued their attack until General William Lambert, the highest ranking officer in the field, ordered it halted.

A Kentuckian later described what he and the other Americans saw: "When the smoke had cleared away, and we had a clear view of the field, it looked at first glance like a sea of blood." The shimmering field was now scarlet with the uniforms of the fallen English.

Then, even as the Americans looked out in wonder on this "sea of blood," the English bodies began to rise before their eyes! With their hands above their heads, more than 500 redcoats surrendered to the Americans. Some had been lightly wounded. Others had been knocked down by cannon blast, or by their retreating comrades.

The English lost 2,000 men—dead, wounded, and captured. The Americans counted seven killed, six wounded on their side. But the battle wasn't over yet.

Gunfire was heard from across the river. British Colonel Thornton, with 1,200 men, had at last reached the American battery. The American troops on the east bank climbed the levee, and tried to see what was happening across the river. All they could see was smoke. But they could *hear* the battle. And what they heard made their hearts sink. The noise of battle was moving upriver toward New Orleans. The Americans on that side were being pushed back.

In fact, the small American force on the west bank, under General David Morgan, did not have much of a chance. Morgan had only 700 men including many Kentuckians without guns. When he could no longer hold his position, he destroyed the cannons and retreated. Marching his men upriver to new positions, Morgan turned around to face the English. He knew that if the English got past him and his men, they could reach a position opposite New Orleans in a few hours. Then they would be able to bring cannons up and shell the city. But as Morgan's men dug in and prepared to face a new attack, night fell.

Thornton knew that the noise of the battle on the east bank had long ago died away. Before pushing on, he decided to ask General Pakenham for further orders.

When the orders came, of course they did not come from Pakenham. They came from General Lambert. He ordered Thornton to march back and recross the river. His majesty's troops had had enough of Louisiana. They were going to get back on their ships and sail away—if only the Americans would let them.

Jackson wanted to attack the English, but other officers talked him out of it. Let the English go, they said. The city had been saved. An attack against the English lines would only needlessly waste American lives.

The English withdrew slowly and carefully, moving by stages from their positions near the battlefield to the shores of Lake Borgne. It wasn't until January 18, 1815 that they finally got on their ships and sailed away.

By that time, though neither the English nor the American troops knew it, the War of 1812 had been over for nearly a month!

CHAPTER 11

The Treaty of Ghent

Back in the early 1800s, news traveled only as fast as a sailing ship or a trotting horse. It took many weeks for news of an event in Europe to cross the Atlantic Ocean to the United States. Because of this, the fight for New Orleans actually took place after the war was officially over. But that didn't mean the battles were unimportant, or fought for nothing.

Peace talks between England and the United States began in August of 1814. The meetings were held in the city of Ghent, Belgium.

When the meetings began, the English expected to win the war easily. They believed their invasion from Canada would succeed, and that they would soon capture New Orleans. The United States would be helpless. She would have no choice but to accept the English demands.

The English representatives began by demanding that the United States give up some of her land. They said that parts of Maine, and some of the land around the Great Lakes, should be given to Canada. And, as if this were not enough, they also insisted that a huge section of the United States should be given to the Indians, for a nation of their own. This Indian nation would contain thousands of square miles, including parts of what are now the states of Indiana, Ohio, Illinois, Wisconsin, and Michigan. The English wanted this Indian nation to remain a constant threat to the United States. It would stop further American growth to the West. And it would be a way of rewarding the Indians for fighting the Americans.

The English representatives demanded even more. They insisted that English ships be allowed to sail up the Mississippi River. This would allow them to take over some of the river trade. It would give Britain complete control of western North America. And it would make it easy to defend the Indians if the Americans continued to take their lands.

The American representatives at Ghent were led by three extremely capable and experienced politicians: John Quincy Adams, Henry Clay, and Albert Gallatin. They were experts at argument, bargaining, and compromises. They gave the English a list of American demands.

Adams was the son of John Adams, the second President of the United States. He himself would go on to become the sixth President. He had been the American ambassador to Russia before being sent to Ghent. Henry Clay was a Kentuckian, and had served both in the Senate and the House of Representatives for many years, though he was only 37 years old. He had been the leader of the "War Hawks" before the war—those who had demanded war with England the loudest. Albert Gallatin was perhaps the most skilled negotiator of them all. He had served in Congress, and for 12 years was Secretary of the Treasury.

Negotiating the peace treaty at Ghent.

He was an expert on banking and finance—and on European politics.

The Americans demanded that Britain promise to stop firing on neutral ships, stop impressing American sailors, and stop trying to tax American trade with Europe. Far from agreeing to give up land to Canada, they insisted that parts of Canada be turned over to the United States.

It was easy to see that the two sides were too far apart. They met for a few weeks, then the meetings broke up. However, both sides stayed in Ghent. They were waiting to see how the war went. Both the English and the Americans knew that if the invasion from Canada succeeded, or if New Orleans were captured, the English would stick to their demands. But if these plans failed, then Britain would face a long war. And the English people were weary of war.

What was really at stake at Ghent was the Louisiana Territory. In their meetings, the English had been careful not to speak about New Orleans or Louisiana. The land they wanted for the Indians was *east* of the Mississippi River, which meant east of the Louisiana Territory. The English said that the Louisiana Purchase had been against international law. If they captured New Orleans, they would sail their ships up the Mississippi River and take control of the whole territory—in the name of Spain, perhaps.

News of the battle on Lake Champlain arrived in Ghent in October. Macdonough's victory meant that invasion from Canada would be held up for a long time. At the suggestion of the English representatives, the talks began again at Ghent.

The English no longer insisted that the United States give up land to Canada, or for an Indian nation. But they would not agree to any of the things the Americans wanted, either. Impressment, the rights of neutral shipping, the taxing of trans-Atlantic trade—these were the things that had caused the United States to go to war in the first place. But the English would agree to nothing on any of these subjects. What they seemed to want was a treaty that said nothing at all!

Adams and the other Americans did not know the English plans. And of course, they had no way of knowing who would win the battle for New Orleans either. But they knew they wanted peace, so an agreement was reached. On December 24, 1814, the Treaty of Ghent was signed. The treaty said only that the two sides would stop shooting at each other. All "disagreements" between the two countries would be settled at some later date.

CHAPTER 12

After The Battles For New Orleans

The first news to reach the east coast of the United States was from New Orleans—Andy Jackson had won! But this news did not arrive until February 4, 1815. A week later an English sloop-of-war sailed into New York harbor. It brought news from Ghent. The war was over.

Soon Americans everywhere were shouting: "Hurray for Peace! Hurray for Andy Jackson!" They didn't care that the issues that caused the war had not been settled. They were only glad that the fighting was over.

They were right to feel as they did. Now that Britain and France were not at war, the issues of impressment, and the searching of American ships by the English, no longer had any importance. And with Jackson's victory at New Orleans, the English hopes of stopping America's growth were destroyed. The "disagreements" the men at Ghent said would be discussed later were simply forgotten.

Nevertheless, the War of 1812 and the battles for New Orleans marked a turning point in American history. Before the war, most Americans thought of their country as a collection of weak and almost independent states huddled together along the Atlantic Ocean. From year to year, the states barely managed to agree to continue as one nation. But the war forced Americans to feel that they were a single people, with a single destiny, and that they had better work together in the future.

The war also made Americans realize that the future they all shared lay in the west. To the Pennsylvania farmer, the Virginia planter, or the Boston merchant, the wilderness across the mountains seemed pretty far away and unimportant. But because so much of the War of 1812 was fought in the West, and especially because of the battles for New Orleans, Americans began to see how important the West was. People began to look beyond the Mississippi to the huge Louisiana Territory that President Jefferson had bought for them. Some people even began to suggest that the United States would one day reach from the Atlantic Ocean to the Pacific, from sea to sea!

In 1812, most Americans were farmers. Most of the things they needed in their daily lives, they could make at home. But for things that had to be made in factories or mills—things like plows or fine cloth—Americans depended on Europe, and especially Great Britain. The war stopped trade with Europe, and then Americans learned they could make manufactured goods themselves. From this small beginning, the United States eventually became the leading manufacturing nation in the world.

The change in how Americans looked upon their country had an effect on politics, too. The New England states and Virginia, which had dominated American politics

As manufacturing boomed, women went to work in factories.

since the American Revolution, lost power.

The western states, like Kentucky and Tennessee, gained in power. Andy Jackson's victory at New Orleans made him the most popular man in the country, and a national hero. He became the leader of the westerners. In 1828, he was elected president, and he was re-elected in 1832. He was the first "frontier" president of the United States.

Neither Britain nor the United States really won the War of 1812. But if there was no winner, there was certainly a loser: the Indians. Their strength east of the Missisippi River was broken. Defeated by General William Henry Harrison in the north, and Jackson in the south, they could no longer hold back the flood of American settlers crossing the mountains. And the defeat of the English at New Orleans took away the only ally that could have helped them.

Again and again in the years that followed, the Indians were driven from their lands. It didn't matter if they had a treaty with the United States promising them the lands. It didn't matter, either, whether they had fought for or against the Americans in the War of 1812. The Choctaws,

Indians watching invasion of their land as settlers move past the Mississippi River.

who were so important in Jackson's victory over the Creeks, and who helped drive the English from New Orleans, received poor reward indeed. Like the other Indian tribes, they were pushed off their land. Eventually the Choctaws were forced to leave all of their lands and travel hundreds of miles to settle in Oklahoma. The man who forced them to make this move was none other than President Andy Jackson!

Because of the victory in the battles for New Orleans, Americans felt that they had won the war of 1812. And this feeling was as important as an actual victory. It gave the Americans more confidence in themselves, and in their young nation. They no longer felt the United States was a small child clutching its mother, Great Britain. The United States was young and healthy—and it was growing.

Historical Places To Visit

Chalmette National Historical Park. This is the site of the battles for New Orleans, eight miles southeast of the city, in the suburb of Chalmette. A white marble monument marks the very spot where the pride of the British army suffered the worst defeat in their history.

Fort McHenry National Monument and Historic Shrine. In Baltimore, Maryland. This is the fort that prevented the English from capturing Baltimore, and which inspired Francis Scott Key's "The Star Spangled Banner."

The Hermitage. Near Nashville, Tennessee. This is the home of Andrew Jackson, defender of New Orleans and 7th President of the United States.

New Orleans. The *Vieux Carré* ("Old Quarter") of New Orleans. Also called "The French Quarter," it is the area bounded by the Mississippi River, Esplanade Ave., Rampart and Canal streets. For the most part, this area is the section of New Orleans that existed in 1814. Many of the buildings that stood then still stand today. At the time of the battles for New Orleans, the city's architecture was beginning to be a mixture of French, Spanish, and "colonial" styles, influenced by Louisiana climate and geography.

Fires in 1788 and 1794 had destroyed most of the earliest buildings, which were crude and not very sturdy anyway. One exception, however, is the *Old Ursuline Convent*, built in 1734, which is French in style and survived the fires.

The old *Place d'Armes*, laid out in 1721, is still the heart of *Vieux Carré*, but it has been renamed *Jackson Square*, with a statue of "Old Hickory" in the center. The ferry across the river is only a few steps away, and the activity of the city's port can be seen from the levee here. Also, only a few steps away is the *Old French Market*, still open for business. Facing Jackson Square is the *Cabildo*, built in 1795 by the Spanish. It was headquarters for the Spanish colonial government. Next door are the *St. Louis*

Cathedral and the *Louisiana Historical Museum,* both dating from before 1800. Another good example of the buildings of that time is a few blocks away, *Lafitte's Blacksmith Shop,* built some time between 1772 and 1791, and believed to have been operated as a blacksmith shop by the Lafitte brothers, Jean and Pierre.

Perry's Victory and International Peace Memorial National Monument. On South Bass Island in Lake Erie, it celebrates Oliver Hazard Perry's naval victory over the English on September 10, 1813, and his famous words: "We have met the enemy, and they are ours."

Plantation homes on the Mississippi. There are more than thirty plantation homes along both sides of the Mississippi River between New Orleans and Baton Rouge, and about a third of them were built before the battles for New Orleans. A visit to these homes will give you some idea of how the wealthiest Creoles and Americans lived in 1814.

INDEX

A

Adams, John, 82
Adams, John Quincy, 82, 85

B

Baltimore, Maryland, 15, 28-29
Barataria Bay, 37, 38, 45
Barbary Pirates, 7, 11
Barron, Commodore James, 7-14, 27
Baton Rouge, Louisiana, 51
Bayou Bienville, 50-51, 75
Bladensburg, Maryland, 27-28, 61
Borgne, Lake, 44, 48, 49, 50, 80
Britain/British. *See* Great Britain
Brown, Noah, 23, 26

C

Canada, 20, 22, 23, 24, 25, 27, 81, 83 84
Caribbean Sea, 31
Carolina, the, 45, 50, 55, 56, 61-62, 69
Carroll, General William, 51
Champlain, Lake, 26, 27, 84
Chesapeake, the, 7, 11-14, 16
Chesapeake Bay, 7, 11, 27, 29
Claiborne, William C., 36-38, 45
Clay, Henry, 82
Cochrane, Vice-Admiral Sir Alexander, 48
Cockburn, Rear Admiral Sir George, 28
Coffee, General James, 51, 55, 57, 78
Creoles, 30-32, 34-36, 37, 38, 42, 44, 52, 58

D

Dickinson, Charles, 40
Downie, Captain George, 26

E

England/English *See* Great Britain
Erie, Lake, 22, 23

F

France, 9, 15, 17, 19, 21, 27, 30, 36, 86

G

Gallatin, Albert, 82-83
"gens de couleur," 31-32, 47, 55
Ghent, Belgium, 81, 82, 83, 84, 86
Ghent, Treaty of, 85
Gibbs, General, 77, 78
Great Britain, 9, 14, 17, 34, 83, 86, 88, 90
    war with France, 9-10, 17-19, 20, 24
    treatment of American ships, 10-11, 17, 86
    threat of war with United States, 11, 14-15, 16-21, 22
    war aims, 24-25
    and American growth, 20-21, 25, 81-82, 84
Gulf of Mexico, 30, 37, 38, 44

H

Hampton, Virginia, 7, 9, 14
Harrison, General William Henry, 23, 89

I

Impressment, 10, 17, 83, 84

Indians, 14, 19-20, 22, 24, 81-82, 88-89
    Creek, 38-39, 90
    Choctaw, 39, 41, 47, 55, 57, 58, 73, 89-90
    Cherokee, 39
    driven from lands, 89-90

J

Jackson, Andrew, 38, 42, 50, 51, 86
    and Indians, 38-39, 89-90
    at Battle of Horseshoe Bend, 39
    early years, 39-40
    duels, 40
    and citizens of New Orleans, 41, 44-47
    description, 44
    at Battles for New Orleans, 53-60, 64-67, 72-75, 80, 86, 87, 88
    plan to burn New Orleans, 60, 64-65
    elected president, 88
Jackson, Rachel, 42
Jamaica, 27, 29, 42, 44
Jefferson, Thomas, 16-17, 20, 21 32, 87
Jones, Lieutenant Ap Catesby, 48-50

K

"Kaintucks," 34, 35, 36, 41
Keane, General, 77, 78
Kentucky, 19, 23, 34, 65, 73, 88
Key, Francis Scott, 28-29

L

Lafitte, Jean, 37-38, 45-47, 50, 62, 69
Lafitte, Pierre, 37
Lake Borgne, 44, 48, 49, 50, 80
Lake Champlain, 26, 27, 84
Lake Erie, 22, 23
Lake Pontchartrain, 44, 50, 72
Lambert, General William, 78, 80
Livingston, Edward, 45-47
Leopard, the, 11-14
Louisiana, the, 45, 50, 61-62, 63, 65, 67
Louisiana Territory, 15, 21, 30, 32, 84, 87

M

Macdonough, Master Commandant Thomas, 26
Madison, Dolley, 28
Madison, James, 21, 28, 38
Maine, 81
Marigny, Bernard, 64-66
McHenry, Fort, 28-29
Mexico, Gulf of, 30, 37, 38, 44
militia, 22, 27, 51, 69
Mississippi River, 21, 25, 30, 33, 34, 50, 51, 55, 62, 72, 75, 76, 77, 82, 84, 87, 88
Mobile (Alabama), 38
Morgan, General David, 79-80

N

Napoleon, 9, 10, 19, 20, 22, 24, 37
Navy, American, 23, 26

Negril Bay, Jamaica, 42-44
Negroes, 31, 33, 47
neutrality, 9
New England, 17, 19, 21, 22, 87
New Orleans, 15, 16, 20, 21, 25, 27, 29, 30-41, 50, 51, 52, 53, 59, 60, 62, 67, 72, 73, 84, 86
  people of, 30-32
  description, 30-31
  Place d'Armes, 34, 43
  English plan attack on, 42-44
  Jackson organizes defenses, 44-47
  Battles for, 50, 53-80, 81, 85, 88, 89, 90
New York, 25, 26, 27, 32
Noble, Jordan, 57

P

Pakenham, General Sir Edward, 60-61, 65, 68-69, 71, 75, 76, 77, 78, 80
Paris, France, 30, 32
Patterson, Master Commandant Daniel, 64
Perry, Commandant Oliver Hazard, 23
Plattsburg, New York, 26
Pontchartrain, Lake, 44, 50, 72
Prevost, General Sir George, 26
Pushmataha, 41

R

riverboats, 33-34, 51
Rodriguez Canal, 55, 57, 59, 61
Ross, Major General Robert, 28

95

S

Santo Domingo, 31, 46, 58
Saratoga, the, 26
Ship and Cat Islands, 48
Spain, 21, 34, 60, 84

T

Tecumseh, 20, 24, 39
Tennessee, 19, 23, 40, 51, 65, 88
Thames River, Battle of, 23-24
Thornton, Col. William, 76, 79-80
Tippecanoe, Battle of, 20
Tonnant, the, 43

V

Villeré Canal, 55, 75
Villeré, Major Gabriel, 51-53
Villeré Plantation, 53, 54

W

"War Hawks," 22, 82
War of American Independence, 9, 19, 21, 40
War of 1812, 21, 31, 43, 80, 86, 87, 88, 89
Washington, D.C., 27-28
Wellington, Duke of, 60
West, the, 19, 22, 34, 82, 87

JAMES PRENDERGAST LIBRARY
Andy Jackson and the battles for New Or[leans]

3 1880 0068321 7

J
973.523   c.1
L   Lyons
           Andy Jackson and the
           battles for New Orleans

Date Due   664

APR 4 1981			

JAMES PRENDERGAST
FREE LIBRARY
JAMESTOWN, NEW YORK
Member Of
Chautauqua-Cattaraugus Library System

PRINTED IN U.S.A.   23-264-002